The Ravens of Castle Keep

Angel Dunworth

> *Dedicated to Mom with lots of love ...*
> *and Rice-a-roni*

This book is a work of fiction. Places, events, and situations in this story are purely fictional. Any resemblance to actual persons, living or dead, is coincidental.

© Copyright 2024 Angel Dunworth.
All rights reserved.

No part of this book may be reproduced, stored in a retrieval system, or transmitted by any means, electronic, mechanical, photocopying, recording, or otherwise, without written permission from the author.

ISBN-13: 978-1-956581-41-6

Canyon Lake, TX

www.ErinGoBraghPublishing.com

Table of Contents

Old Ghosts 1
Werewolves and White Gravy 10
Many Past Lives 17
Thirsty Tricks... 28
Miracles or Madness................................. 34
The Contraption and the Ghost 41
Bird Doctors 55
Sink or Swim 63
Cloak and Dagger Stuff............................ 72
Ryan's Ravens 79
Stairway to Heaven?................................. 85
Bully 91
All good things 101
The End... 105
About the Author 106

1
OLD GHOSTS

There was a knock at our door, that felt empty and cold... it felt like a monster was knocking. It was worse than that.

A knock at the door is usually fun. A friend, a school mate. It's exciting when you think someone's come to play video games. But when you open the door and it's a police man saying, "I have some bad news" All the fun goes away.

"There's been a horrible car accident," the police man told us. He said that Mom had been injured. He told us that she probably wouldn't live. People with brain injuries rarely do.

Even after he left the house, I felt like everything was gone. I still feel like that.

It seems like that knock happened a million years ago. It was only one year ago. Facebook had posted the memory of it. I don't want to remember.

The car accident happened a few weeks before my birthday. I told Dad to cancel the party too. I couldn't celebrate anything.

The two of us were in the hospital waiting on news, every second of every day. When the doctors told us that Mom was talking, I got really excited! I felt like, her being able to speak was a birthday present just for me. But then we went to her bedside. No matter what we said she just responded, "It was a summer day. There was an accident."

And it's been like that ever since. I think it left a bunch of holes in me. Like I couldn't breathe right anymore. Like somebody was sitting on my chest.

It never, ever changes.

"Mom, it's me Marcy. Do you remember me?"

"It was a summer day. There was an accident."

"Mom, do you still like the color red?"

"It was a summer day. There was an accident."

"Mom, how can you hate me enough to forget my name?"

"It was a summer day. There was an accident."

"Mom, are the bills paid? Does the stove work? What if I put peanut butter in my shoes and do cartwheels on the roof?"

"It was a summer day. There was an accident."

The doctors said it's not uncommon for people with this kind of injury to never speak again… or to remain in a coma. They said that we should be grateful that she's alive. I tried to be. But I wasn't important enough to her, that she'd remember me.

So awhile back I stopped visiting.

Dad did his best, but traveling all the time for work, made me miss a lot of school. He didn't want to leave me at home, all by myself. I know I've only just turned 12, but I think I could've handled myself all by myself.

Still, I have no complaints at the moment. That's because Dad's sending me to a castle, to be schooled by a "school marm" type! A teacher that has only one other student right now. I was wishing for a girl roommate, like a make best friends' kind of thing. It's a little boy though. Just an eight-year-old. I guess that'll be okay.

A castle! A real one! I've always wanted to be a ghost-hunter! Every castle has a ghost. And best of all I can avoid visiting Mom every week. I'll be too busy with spooky research! Maybe I can do all my essays on ghosts!

I think this is the first time I've been excited about anything since Mom got hurt.

That's almost like a ghost, a really bad one that haunts me every minute. It's like she had the accident but we suffered. Maybe hurting is one sort of ghost, but that kind of ghost should stay buried.

"My name's Ryan," a rather round boy with a face full of freckles tells me. I introduce myself, then go quiet. As soon as we arrived a scary looking old lady, named Mrs. Krench led us up to the library. She looked like a witch from a fairy tale or something. She had a wart and all. She yelled at us to sit still and not to touch anything.

Then the old witch laughs like a donkey, "Bra-ha-haw". She slams the door behind her.

"That old lady? Was she a wicked witch?" the boy says reading my thoughts.

"I thought so. But why do you think so?" I'm asking him mostly because a true ghost-hunter has to be thorough.

"Cuz she looks like the picture in my Nan's fairy book about Snow White." he says plain.

"She *so* does!" I agree and we giggle.

"This castle used to have tours my Nan said. I really thought we'd get one," he tells me.

At that moment, a woman smashes the door open and barges to our table. She looks young, but not real. She looks like she came from a story book.

"Why are you dressed like that?" I blurt. She's wearing a long skirt, boots and a white blouse with bunches of lace at her throat. She doesn't fit in 'now'... she looks like she drives a horse-drawn carriage.

"Rude child!" she snips, "But yes, I can see why our costumes here would seem odd to the outside world. My name is Ms. Priscilla and I am your teacher."

"Hi. Mrs. Priscilla," Ryan yelps.

"Ms." she retorts, "NOT Mrs!"

"You aren't dressed like a teacher. All my teachers wear jeans and stuff," Ryan tells her and I nod my agreement.

"Well, once you have studied you too will be wearing costumes. The Castle Keep was once kept alive by tourist dollars. People, though very few, still take the tour sometimes. It is important that though they may be touring the public half of the castle, that if they see any who live here, we are dressed in a historic costume. Any time period is allowed. I decided my costume should be from the Victorian Era, but you two might enjoy Medieval... princesses and knights? You will decide at the end of the school year." she informs us, and I get kind of excited just then.

What a fun teacher, I think. But I am immediately corrected.

"First term you may decide what you most want to study, with any of your remaining, required classes starting next term. So, think for a moment. What do you most want to know?" she asks merrily.

We look at each other, blank.

"Think on it tonight. For now, Mr. Headly, our groundskeeper, will give you the tour of the public half of our home. Afterwards go to the kitchen and learn your chores."

"CHORES?" We both screech. I've never heard of a teacher giving chores.

"Yes. You are to help Mrs. Krench with the kitchen work. You will need to know how to cook for yourselves one day. There's no better way or time to learn." she says rather coldly.

Then she leaves.

"I hope this isn't our classroom," Ryan says.

"Why not?" I sort of wonder, but really, I'm keeping an eye out for the castle ghost. *We're in the library.... Ghosts can read. Right?*

"There are no computers. No tablets?" he says.

I think about it. I say, "There was no TV in my room, now that you mention it."

"Mine either," he agrees.

"It's a big place. We'll find them eventually," I assure him.

Old Mr. Headly, the grounds keeper, is the only person not in a costume, probably because he has mud and scratches from head to toe. If he ever gets a costume, it should be Santa because he has a long white beard… it's so fuzzy you can barely see his face.

He's the nicest old man I ever met. As soon as we got to the other side of the castle (where Ms. Priscilla couldn't see) he asked if we wanted sweeties. We never heard that before. He gave us each a lollipop. I don't really eat those, but it was still really nice of him.

He showed us around, told us lots of stuff about castles. He even showed us a waterway that ran through the floor of a tiny room under the castle. It looked like there was a little door under the water. He told us they used to use it to keep food cold before there were refrigerators.

Unfortunately, he also told us the only "newer technology" in the castle was the electric, plumbing and heaters. We asked about computers, cell-phones, a bunch of stuff. He told us these things weren't allowed in the castle. He told us the kitchen had a land-line for emergencies. I don't really know what that is though. The kitchen phone looks like an alien spaceship to me.

"Aye, it seems strange to ya kids." he told us, "But it makes sense from history's eyes. Used to have tours every day. Kept the place runnin', now... castle's goin' broke. Skint to the bone.'"

"It's not going to close, is it? I don't want to go back to my old school." Ryan informs him.

"Time will out," Mr. Headly says, "I worked here since I were a young, young man. Maybe a million years ago." And then he winks and we all giggle.

"Rode me a T-rex to work back then." he tells us.

"Nah!" I laugh, "That's impossible. How old are you really?"

"As old as me bones and older than me teeth," he jokes.

But our laughter ends as we are called to the kitchen by a fussy cook that looks like an old witch!

*Birds (and animals) mourn their dead.
Crows have been seen sitting beside their
dead companions for days, as if keeping a vigil.*

2
WEREWOLVES AND WHITE GRAVY

"Maybe Mrs. Krench is an old witch," I tell Ryan as we head up the stairs to bed, "But she can cook for me anytime!"

"I know!" he chirps, "And did you see how she just added flour and made the white gravy? It was like a magic trick. This is WAY better than my last school."

"What was wrong with your last school?" I wonder aloud.

"Bullies. I got beat-up every single day." he tells me sadly.

"Wait! Your parents paid gobs of money because of bullies? Instead of going to the principal?" I ask.

"No," he winces, "My Nan. I live with my Nan… but… She's starting to get sick. So instead of an inheritance she gave her life savings to keep me here, until I graduate."

"I'm really sorry to hear it," I tell him solemnly. "Looks like we have something in common. My Mom's sick too."

"That's awful,' he says, "I know how bad it feels."

I feel okay for a few minutes after he says that. Since Mom's accident my insides have felt like electricity and claws. But for right now at least, my insides feel okay.

Do I feel better because he understands? I ask myself but myself doesn't answer.

He asks out of the blue, "What are you gonna ask to study tomorrow?"

"How to hunt ghosts!" I smile. I think it's smart really, "No textbooks. Just essays on my findings."

"Ooohhh," he replies, "That's a great idea. Maybe I'll ask to be a wizard."

"Perfect!" I say as I open my bedroom door, "MS. Priscilla will see just who she's dealing with!"

I start to close the door with a good-night. Ryan sputters, "Um. Wait."

"What?" I ask confused.

"Will you walk me to my room? Just this once? I don't want to get lost."

"Lost?" I mumble, "You've been in and out of your room all day."

"I… it's dark now. Everything looks different." he replies and I see him going pale. I realize he's afraid of the dark and so I walk him to his room down the hall. I even open his door and flick the lights on before he enters.

He smiles, "If you ever need a bestest friend I can be a good one."

I say goodnight and go to my room.

I was sleeping really well until I felt a nudge. I jump awake and there stands Ryan at my bedside. He yelps, "Can I sleep in here?"

"Are you crazy?" I ask, but I see that he is shaking, "Ryan, what's wrong?"

"Werewolves are gonna eat me! Help Marcy! Please!" he screeches.

"What? Did you have a nightmare?" I ask.

But then I hear it.

Howling in the darkness. The sound turns to ice and goes up my spine. I cough nervously.

Howling.

I try hard to listen. Is it just one howl?

No.

In a few minutes it sounds like a whole bunch of werewolves howling together. I feel so scared. I don't want Ryan to know I'm scared because it might make him even more terrified. (And he's so little.)

"Okay," I mutter, "I'll sleep on that weird couch. There's strength in numbers… I don't think werewolves eat more than one person a day. So, if we stay together, we'll be fine."

"Lounge," he says.

"What?" I ask confused.

"The weird couch. It's called a lounge," he says, but as I take the blanket, he fusses at me, "I need the blanket. It's cold."

"No. It's my blanket. Use the sheet." I insist.

I climb onto the lounge but I can't sleep. Howling, howling and more howling. The room seems darker. The shadows get thick like molasses. If I could utter a sound, I think I'd actually scream. My throat is so tight I can't even swallow. My chest is banging in my ears.

After a few more endless minutes, I finally hear Ryan start to snore.

Why did I tell Ryan we'd be safe together? He should be standing guard like me, I think.

I get all my courage together. I tip-toe over to the window. I open the wooden shudders. They give an eerie CREEEEEEK sound.

I'm so frightened now that my goosebumps have goosebumps.

Ghosts, please ghosts, please, please not werewolves. I beg God.

I look at the moon. It's not a full moon. I decide that werewolves only eat people on full moons. I don't really know though. I never believed in werewolves until this very second, so I don't really know anything about them.

It seems like hours and hours before I fall asleep.

Ryan and I lived through the night, but maybe wished we hadn't. Ms. Priscilla bashes my door open in the morning. She is so angry. My tummy hurts… that's how upset she looks. I think I'm afraid of her, maybe as much as werewolves.

"Boys are not allowed in girl's quarters! That normally means instant expulsion!" she screams.

Ryan and I look at each other. I can see he's ready to cry. He can't go back to his Nan, so where would he go? Being expelled is seriously bad in a regular school. But it might be worse here.

She sees our faces and adds, "But since you are still new, you will be given a chance to explain your obvious disregard for the rules."

"We were hiding from the werewolves!" Ryan blurts.

Ms. Priscilla scoffs. Her voice goes flat and nasal, "Are you kidding me?'

"I heard them too! Why else would I let him stay?" I yelp.

"The trouble with your answer is that there's no such thing. I am disappointed in you two." she gripes.

"We are telling the truth. Why are you disappointed?" I screech angrily.

"Because you are not telling the truth. Instead, you are telling yourselves a lie. First lesson: when the unbelievable happens think on the believable."

"What's that supposed to mean?" Ryan asks.

"If werewolves aren't real, then you must ask yourself if something that IS real could make the same sound, howling. Use your logic. What else, besides werewolves' howl?" she asks.

"Well, coyotes? Dogs sometimes. Regular zoo wolves? Wolves howl together." I answer.

"Whoa!" Ryan says with his eyes lighting up, "You have real live wolves here?"

"Yes. They live in the forest just past the small moors. They are federally protected here. The townsfolk see them as a mascot. However, if you see one do not approach it. It may have whelps it is protecting. If so…. It may bite to keep it's young safe."

"Is that why the town is called New Wolveston?" I ask.

"Yes. Now… you've broken the rules, though expulsion may be a bit harsh. Instead, you will peel potatoes during your free hour. I think any punishment harsher than that might be unfair."

"I dunno how to peel potatoes," Ryan yelps.

"Learn!" she commands and is gone.

3
Many Past Lives

We sit in the library waiting for the teacher to arrive. Poor Ryan has little band-aides on every finger from misusing the potato peeler. I finally got him doing it correctly, but it took a while.

And even with Ryan being hurt, Mrs. Krench, the old witch was mean. She kept telling him that nobody wants bloody potatoes.

Then she laughed her donkey laugh, "Bra-ha-haw!" I hate her.

I try to comfort Ryan while we wait for Ms. Priscilla.

"At least this way we get hash browns with breakfast," I say hoping to cheer him up.

"No… those were potatoes," he says.

"Well, yeah. Hash browns are just shredded fried potatoes." I respond.

"Oh? I always thought they were fried hash," he tells me.

"Hash?"

"Yeah, you know, corned beef."

It is about this time that Ms. Priscilla makes her boisterous entrance. I dunno why she's always so loud when she's opening doors. She tells us that every morning while we wait for her, we have to journal. It doesn't matter what we write about, as long as we write.

Finally, she asks the "big" question. I feel so excited! Like maybe I outsmarted her!

"What do you most want to learn about?"

"Ghosts!" I announce and I wait for her to tell me she doesn't know anything about it. I know she'll tell me she has to learn too.

It's perfect. It ought to fix her annoying attitude about werewolves! I hate peeling potatoes.

Something is wrong. I tell her I want to learn about ghosts. She doesn't bat an eye.

When Ryan says he wants to be a wizard, she doesn't even get upset!

Instead, she hands us each books, piles of books. Not even magic books. Textbooks! I see she's given me history and literature and before I can even complain she tells me, "History is filled with ghosts. As such you must clear away the ghosts to find the truth."

"How?" I ask, kinda snippy. *I wanted to find real ghosts! She tricked us.*

"There are three versions of every time period in all of history. There is the version written by the conquerors. There is the version written by the conquered. Somewhere in the middle, where both accounts match you will likely find a better picture of the truth." she tells me. She hands me a book written by a child who grew-up in an Indian school.

"First account," she says, then she hands me a slim book. It's filled mostly with newspaper articles about Indian schools opening. She says, "Second account. Compare these, fact check, and then write a five-page essay about the contrasts and what you believe is closest to the truth. If either of you need to do more research there is a computer at the library in town. Just ask Mr. Headly and he'll drive you up."

She leaves the room and Ryan yelps, "Stupid books on science and old Roman machines and stuff? I said I wanted to be a wizard!"

"Yeah. She's mean." I agree.

But a minute later Ryan shows me a diagram in one of his books. In order to measure a space for building, the Romans had made a long string with measurements on it. They would tie it to an arrow and shoot it to the other side of where they were building. Then they'd just look at the number of feet. That's how they measured things.

Ryan yelps, "Hey! That's really cool. How did they figure it out?"

I want to keep complaining. This stupid teacher gave me history and literature, my two worst subjects! I have to stop complaining. My friend is looking through his new book with ooohhs and ahhs.

It just makes me mad.

I guess he's on her side now.

Lessons come and go.

The Indian School essay got an A+ anyway. There were lots of awful accusations on the internet, so bad that I didn't use any of those. I wrote about the Native kids learning trades. I explained how it sort of ruined everything. They had a bunch of skills but nothing that could help on the Reservations where their families were. For instance, learning to resole shoes isn't something people who wear moccasins need. They all just faded into the new society, where their skills might earn a living. It was really sad though because they were all renamed and so even brother and sister might never find each other again.

I was proud when I got a good grade. But now everything seems weirdly numb. I think I will actually die of boredom.

No TV, no video games, no social media or even old movies! I almost hate our free hours. We can only have Mr. Headly take us into town if the castle library has no books on what we are researching for school. Even then the library in town has only one computer, so we have to share it. We don't have any extra time to use it for more than homework either.

I'm still on the lookout for ghosts but I haven't seen any. My literature book is all ghost stories, but they scare me. It's not doing much for my confidence. How can I ever be a ghost-hunter and be afraid of ghosts? I think maybe I want to live somewhere else. I'd miss Ryan, but he's really being weird. I can't explain it.

We each get $5 a week and we ride into town every weekend. It's for fun. We always go to the candy store. But there's something weird going on. Last week Ryan didn't want candy. He asked Mr. Headly to take him to the hardware store. He showed me he'd bought a bunch of cogs. COGS! Not cogs made of sugar, real metal cogs like they use in clocks! Maybe the boredom made him go crazy. I'm not sure!

In the middle of me reading my homework in Literature, *August Heat*, which is crazy scary, Ryan bursts into my room. He doesn't even knock. I start to yell at him but he looks frazzled, really afraid.

"Come with me! Somebody's dead," he screeches.

"What? Calm down!" I beg. I keep trying to calm him but he keeps yelling someone's dead.

He is pulling me up the tower stairs a few minutes later. Really hard. I'm tripping up the stairs, begging him to calm down. I can see Ms. Priscilla at the bottom of the stairwell. She is just starting to climb as I am pulled round a corner and onto a rooftop.

Ryan screams hysterically, "That giant monster bird killed somebody! He's got a bone!"

"Birds don't kill people," I try to reassure him, but he keeps screaming, "I came up here to try to invent something. But then that bird flew up with a bone!"

A big black bird sits quietly on the wall... a bone in his beak. He's as big as an eagle. It's kinda scary. Why on earth would a bird have a bone? It's not like you could build a nest with it.

"Listen! I don't think birds kill people!" I respond.

"Well then why does it have a bone?" he studders a little, "More... m... more are coming!"

Ms. Priscilla stands outside of the doorway on the roof now. She says, "When things are impossible, think on the possible. These birds are ravens, Ryan. They eat the carrion left by the wolves."

"What's a carrion?" he asks alarmed, but much calmer.

"Well, it's a carcass. Let's say the wolves hunt and eat a sheep. But there is too much to eat all of it. The carcass, the scraps, that's what ravens live off of. They are nearly always friends with wolf packs. You'll see a lot of crows up here as well. Smaller birds, but also black.'

"So? They kind of clean-up the yucky stuff? Nature's trash?" I ask.

"Exactly!" she reassures us. "And the more you get to know them, the more astounded you will become at their absolute brilliance! One university is claiming that they are the smartest birds on earth."

I guess it's important because she says, "Right! Two less hours of book lessons. You are both to observe these birds and report all discoveries!"

After she leaves Ryan yelps happily, "Pets!"

I'm not sure he understands the assignment.

Corvids are omnivorous. This means they eat meat, plants and bugs. Ravens in particular seem to eat just about anything.

Mrs. Krench shows us the pot again. She says, "Then ya just drop in the rest of these vegetables and a bit of flour. But it ain't a soup. It's a stew. Ya hear?"

"What's the difference?" Ryan asks.

"Difference is ya stew it! Whatdya think it's called a stew for?" she snaps at him.

"Well, how do you stew it?" I snap. It's not that I care to learn this.

She snapped at Ryan, so I'm snapping at her! I think.

"Bra-ha-haw! You turn the heat low and let it cook a real long while," she tells me.

"How long is that?" Ryan asks.

"Til it's done! What else?" she yelps.

She's not much of a teacher. The only lesson I understood is how to make pancakes. Luckily, we are excused. Mr. Headly opens the door and asks, "Ye kids wanna go to town? I gotta get supplies."

"Bra-ha-haw! Naw. No. They ain't meant to leave today!" Mrs. Krench snaps, "That head mistress will be fit to be tied!"

"Bugger that!" Mr. Headly replies, "I been working these grounds 30 some odd years. She only been here four!"

We leave them to argue. We are already in the truck when Mr. Headly arrives.

He says low, "I need ye help." He hands us piles of papers that advertise the castle.

"You want us to hand these out? Like advertising tours of the castle?" I ask.

"Yeah. There's a rich land owner, Mr. Rigby. He's tryin' to take over the castle's debt." he says sadly.

"Isn't that good?" I ask.

"Naw. He's fixin' to knock it all down. Wants to build a mini mall there."

"He can't do that," Ryan replies a tear running down his cheek, "My Nan said if the castle closes, I'll be put in a state-home!"

"Is that true?" I screech. My throat is so tight I can't get the words out properly. I'm almost crying too.

"Aye," he says sadly, "Foster care or orphanage."

After a long silence he adds, "Some of those places is nice though. Toys, a bed, nice people. New sisters and brothers."

"NO." Ryan shouts angrily, "I don't need sisters. I got Marcy. A bestest friend is better than a stupid sister!"

I want to be sick. I want to scream, "Unfair" until my lungs fall out. I want to fix it. I want to make Ryan safe. But all I can do is hold his hand. I really hope that's enough.

Ravens are birds that are classified as Corvids. There are 135 different species of Corvids. Crows, Magpies, Jackdaws, Rooks, Jays, Treepies, Choughs and Nutcrackers are other birds that are a part of the Corvid family.

4
Thirsty Tricks

This morning came with high hopes. We saw tours going into the public part of the castle. Maybe it'll be okay. Later we went to the kitchen to get scraps for the birds, but the scraps were almost nothing. I found some walnuts that are in the shell, but I don't know if ravens eat nuts.

Ryan is carrying his bottle of water in case the birds are thirsty. We've been giving them food scraps all week. There's usually about five ravens and a couple of crows. The crows are building a nest because there's lots of food here.

I had wondered aloud, "Why did they build it low? I mean why did they build their nest under an under-hang? Why didn't they build their nest of the top of a turret?"

"Rain?" Ryan asked, "The under-hang is like a roof. To keep the babies dry, maybe?"

"Wow! You're brilliant!" I tell him, "I'd have never thought of that!"

We named the biggest raven, Joe. I give him a walnut. The shell was still on. I doubt he'll eat it. It's impossible to eat with the shell on. Isn't it?

He astounds us. The raven takes the nut to the corner, where Mr. Headly had left a few bricks when he repaired the roof.

Joe drops his walnut on the ground. He picks up a piece of brick with his beak and one talon, and drops it on the walnut. When he removes the brick, the nut has cracked. It lays broken and Joe can eat the insides. My mouth is hanging open.

"Cool!" Ryan cheers, "Marcy, they can't drink the water out of this bottle. What do I do?"

I find some old buckets that Mr. Headly left. Exploring them I see powders in most of them.

But if someone is mixing concrete in buckets they need water, I think. I finally find an old pitcher. It is smaller than the buckets. Perhaps Mr. Headly was using it to bring extra water for his concrete? It's small in width, but at least it's clean.

I decide that as long as it's clean it must be safe to use. "Pour your water in here. It doesn't look like Mr. Headly used it for concrete or anything." I offer.

He pours it into the small pitcher, but there isn't enough water. It's only about two or three inches deep, even after I'd also poured my water bottle into it.

"It's not enough!" Ryan yelps, "They can't get the water out. It's too low. Their heads are even too big to fit inside of it."

Joe and another raven, named Hadley (After nice Mr. Headly) make a loud "Caw."

"You see?" Ryan whimpers, "Even they know they can't get it."

We watch as Joe and his closest friend (who we named Paddy) begin picking up pebbles and rocks and dropping them into the bucket.

"See?" Ryan gripes, "We insulted them. They're throwing rocks in there! Dirty old rocks!"

But this trouble will have to wait because the bell rings for class.

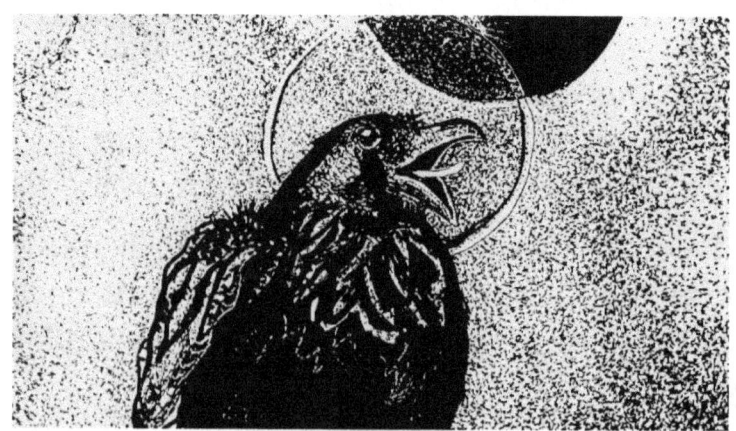

Studies show that the first thing a bird or animal seeks out when claiming territory is an easily accessed water source.

After class we report to the kitchen. We are surprised to find Mr. Headly there. He's peeling apples. He has a big dish of them in front of him.

"Where's the wicked…" Ryan begins but I cut him off, "Where's Mrs. Krench?"

"She be ill. Had to drop her at hospital. I'm sure ya kids noticed the tumor on her face. So, I guess it ain't no secret." he tells us. I can see his eyes welling with tears.

"You mean the wart? I thought it was a wart on her face," I yelp. I feel so tiny. So cruel. So evil, as if I'm the worst person ever. I'm so sorry for calling her names that I start to cry.

It wasn't a wart! It was a tumor! It was cancer! That truth fills me with horrible pain. Pain that weighs my head down. It's what the Indian school book called, *lose your face in shame*. I know exactly what that means now.

"We've been calling her a witch? And the whole time she had cancer?" I howl. I am angry, sad, scared and confused all at the same time. I think I might burst.

I see the truth flicker on in Ryan's eyes. His face drops. I wish he was too small to understand. Then he'd feel safe. For some weird reason we are suddenly both bullies for calling Mrs. Krench names.

We are just as bad as the bad things we went through now. Aren't we?

"Go lay down," Ryan instructs me, "I'll make dinner. She won't have to cook anymore. She can just rest. I'll make dinner from now on."

He is promising for real. He is making some sacred oath that he cannot break. Somehow, we all know that. We know he's not really old enough. Still, the way he said those words, not in regret or sympathy, but as if to atone, as if to right the wrongs. That thought is so clear that we can all feel it inside our own hearts

Someone should say a few words. Someone should say whatever would make his eight-year-old heart feel okay. But his oath is so solemn that nobody speaks.

I have to admit that dinner was pretty good! Ryan and Mr. Headly made a ham with cinnamon apples. And the sides were only things Ryan could make by himself, so we had canned peas and pancakes with white gravy. It was actually delicious.

After dinner Ms. Priscilla announced that Mrs. Krench's doctors feel very positive she'll fully recover. She's gone to live with her sister until she's well. Until then a replacement cook will take over.

I really think Ryan was relieved. Ms. Priscilla even told him that he'd got an A+ in cooking.

But the best was yet to come. I have such amazing news for Ryan that I'm nearly bursting.

I know why Joe and Paddy threw rocks in the pitcher!!

I can't show him until tomorrow when we visit them on the rooftop. Some secrets are so hard to keep.

Scientists claim that crows are as intelligent as a seven-year-old child.

5
Miracles or Madness

On the way to the roof, I am bursting. Ryan saved apple peels and a pancake for the birds. I've only brought a couple of bottles of water. But I also have a very special secret! He will be truly amazed!

Ryan looks at me once we reach the rooftop. He gives me a look of disgust.

"You only brought two water bottles? Why? It's not enough!" he screeches.

Joe flies close to Ryan, landing in front of him. He bows his head and makes a sort of wince and clicking sound. Ryan stands there a minute. Joe nudges him gently and again makes the noise, bowing his head. Ryan must be quite brave because even with Joe's long, sharp beak he touches Joe's neck and gives him a scratch. Joe repeats the sound and returns to the wall.

We smile at each other.

"Marcy, did you see? He likes me."

"Of course he likes you. But come here because they're thirsty." I respond merrily.

He walks to where I am. He lets out a moan and looks angry. He tells me, "They're mad, I guess. They filled the water pitcher with rocks!"

"Yeah! But just wait til you see why. Here. You pour the water in." I say as I hand him the water bottles. He looks at me confused but he opens the first bottle. He pours in the water. With all of the rocks beneath it the water level has risen high enough for the birds to drink.

"They couldn't reach the water. So, they put the rocks in the bottom of the pitcher to bring the water up to them!" I yelp excitedly.

"Whoa!" Ryan screeches, "My book Ms. Priscilla gave me said that cavemen weren't really smart enough to create any kind of civilization until they learned to use tools!"

'So?" I say as this reaction was not what I expected.

"They know how to use tools! The rocks are tools for the water. Cracking walnuts with bricks. The brick is a tool! That's amazing!"

"Yeah," I agree, "Especially the pitcher. I would've died of thirst!"

Suddenly he looks like someone stole his heart. He mutters quietly, "I never want to leave here. What if they sell the castle? We'd never see Joe again."

"Try not to worry," I say low, "As long as people are touring the place we'll be okay."

But part of me has already noticed that the tourists are visiting less and less. I don't have the heart to say it though.

Ravens have a language of their own, Scientists put the number of varying calls at approximately 33 different calls.

I ended up going into town alone for my free time this weekend. I knock on Ryan's door **a lot**... but for the last two weeks he just yells that he's busy. It's annoying.

I had a great idea. Mr. Headly and I made up fliers that say, "Save the Castle" We even got a couple of donations! It wasn't much though. It was only enough for a couple of months or so.

My Dad called last night, but I told Ms. Priscilla I had a tummy ache from dinner. I really didn't feel like talking to him. I used to have a real home with him and Mom. That's gone. I have a new home, a family of birds. I doubt he'd understand that those birds... they kill all of the pain. We never know what new trick they'll do. And that makes me feel like there's a future. I have something to look forward to again.

Ms. Priscilla talked to him. My Dad told her that in about a month I have to visit my mother. He'll be in Singapore (wherever that is) so she'll have to take me. It'll be my mother's birthday.

Who cares? I don't care! Why should I? She's not going to know it's her birthday. She won't even notice me there. So why should I go?

It's almost insulting because the birds on the rooftop know who I am. They make happy "Caws" whenever they see me. Even when I'm on the ground and they're flying. They never say "It was a summer day. There was an accident."

They can't talk English but they make me know they love me! Why can't she? Just once, just one more time to call me, her sweet baby girl. Just once. I know she could if she wanted to because that's only three words. Probably way easier to say than two whole sentences.

I wanted to talk to Ryan about it, but I guess he's hiding in his room. They say his Nan's getting worse. At least he knows his Nan loves him. Maybe I'd hide too though. I dunno.

Instead of the candy store I go to the library. I use the computer to find a video on ravens and crows. The man on the video says they're corvids. The video shows this enormous puzzle. The birds have to figure out how to get a small stick, then use the stick to get a treat. The birds know how! They figure the whole puzzle out! First, they pull the stick off of a string, then place it in a sort of box and pull out the treat! It's so cool!

I am truly amazed. But how did they know? Were they trained? I find other videos about the same thing. These birds are so incredibly smart. They can figure out the puzzles that the scientists put out, even when the objects are moved around.

They even figure out more complex puzzles that are much harder! Wow!

Before my time expires on the computer, I look up Castle Keep. Just for kicks because I have less than three minutes of computer time left. (And also, for ghost stories. Maybe I'll get lucky.)

I gasp. There's actually a video! I turn it on. It's some rough looking guy. I've never seen him before. He keeps showing blueprints and pictures of the castle. He keeps insisting that the lost treasure of the castle was sealed up inside the walls.

Wait! Treasure?

There's a treasure in the castle?

I've never heard that before.

He tells his audience, "This is one of the largest recorded treasures in history."

Really? I gasp. *That much gold could probably save the castle! It could pay the debt!*

The man says, "The only place that this much gold could be hidden is within the massive walls of Castle Keep."

I get very excited!

But then he says something that makes my chest hurt. He assures the viewers that, "I will stop at nothing to get this treasure."

As he says, "Subscribe" I begin to wonder who this guy is.

I look under the video to find out the man's name, "Nathan Rigby. Rigby?" That's the guy who wants to knock the castle down! Now I know why!

None of this is about a mini-mall! He's not trying to make more jobs or anything like that! All of this is about a missing treasure! Rigby's not really interested in building new businesses. He just wants the treasure for himself!

BUT if me and Ryan get to it first, the castle is saved!

Crows and ravens make their homes everywhere across the globe. They are highly adaptable in this respect.

6
The Contraption and the Ghost

I've told everyone about the treasure. Nobody seems excited. Mr. Headly said, "Aye. It were a rumor started for bringing tours in. I been here thirty odd years. If there were treasure I'da found it."

Despite his assurance that there is no treasure, today before I went to see the birds, I took every book off of the bookshelf in my room to see if there was a secret door that led to the treasure (like in movies.) I had no luck and had to put them all back. Until now I'd never noticed how heavy books are.

Even Ryan doesn't seem to care about lost treasure. But I can tell that he's bursting to tell me something.

"I'm better than a wizard! I'm an inventor!" he tells me during breakfast. He continues to tell me that he's invented something over and over, but when pressed can't tell me what.

It doesn't matter that he doesn't want to be a wizard. I've given up on ghosts! I think as I remember how scared I got last night reading my literature book.

I can't hunt ghosts while running away from them. Can I?

When we get to the rooftop all of our birds are waiting. Except Joe. We look at each other. Joe being missing might be a bad sign.

Ryan sits and starts setting up his invention. Suddenly we hear Mrs. Krench laughing.

"Bra-ha-haw"

I stand and look for her. She's not here.

Ryan is turning white.

"Did she die? Is she a ghost now?" he begs and looks to be crying.

"Bra-ha-haw" we hear again. I shake my head. I run to the stairwell door. It has to be her idea of a joke.

"She's probably back," I yelp as I pull open the door. Nothing. No one. Mrs. Krench isn't here.

"Bra-ha-haw Bra-ha-haw," we hear again. Now I think we both have turned white.

"A ghost?" I stammer, but then I think for a moment. From the look on Ryan's face, he's trying to do the same.

He whimpers, "When things are impossible, think on the possible."

He says this over and over, but the laughter becomes louder.

"Bra-ha-haw" we shudder at the sound.

"Bra-ha-haw Bra-ha-haw" we feel like we've turned to ice.

I have to think of something to calm Ryan down. He looks like he's gonna be sick.

At that moment I remember something from the ghost stories, "Quoth, the raven, 'Nevermore.'"

"What?" Ryan brays behind the scary "Bra-ha-haw"

"It's a ghost story," I tell him, "In my book. A guy goes crazy because this raven keeps saying one word. That's the possible! Ravens can mimic!"

As if on cue Joe swoops down and lands on the wall. He opens his beak and says, "Bra-ha-haw"

We are so relieved.

Then Paddy flies up and drops a stick at our feet.

"Awww" Ryan says, "Thanks Paddy."

"It's a thank you!" I crow.

"Yeah!" Ryan agrees, "Like he's paying for his treats!"

A few minutes later Ryan sets up his invention. It's just some plastic hamster tubes, boxes and cogs. He shows me how it works. He puts food in the top, a little bite of ham, which is Joe's favorite. If Joe drops a pebble onto a lever, it moves the cogs and drops the food.

Joe is very interested. He caws in a few different pitches. The first time Ryan works his mechanism it works perfectly. However, when Joe tries it something inside of it gets stuck.

Joe is undaunted. He picks up the stick and digs out the food from the top plastic tube of the thing. He eats it with a loud "Caw-ka-caw".

"It might need some work," Ryan admits.

Did you know that Corvids are not the only birds who can mimic? Parrots and Grackles are also examples of mimics.

Angel Dunworth

"The Raven" is a spooky poem written by Edgar Allen Poe. Poe was an American poet/writer who was born in Boston in the 1800's. He is still considered one of the world's most prolific writers today. Quoth the raven...

Things with the treasure had started to look-up. For a short while Ryan was helping me look. We pushed a lot of loose bricks in the castle's walls to see if a secret-passage opened anywhere. We had no luck, but we had high hopes. Until...

The very worst thing happened to Ryan...

His Nan died. I feel awful for Ryan. I was a lot more worried about him than I thought. When his Nan was only sick, that was like a bond I shared with Ryan. Like an ugly thing that perfectly connected us.

I never thought about it actually happening. But then it did.

When Ms. Priscilla told us, I think I died for a moment. It felt like a giant, boulder fell onto my chest. And I think Ryan felt the boulder too, because he fell flat onto the floor. He fell on his face; I didn't know what to do. I thought he was hurt. I tried to pick him up off of the floor. He seemed to be fighting to stay there. Then I heard him wailing, deeper than any ghost ever could.

Ms. Priscilla told me to go to my room for a while, so that Ryan could be alone. She stayed with him, patting his back. She didn't try to make him move from the floor. As I left, I could hear her singing softly to him.

I didn't tell anyone, but I can sometimes hear Ryan crying at night.

That was a few weeks ago. He rarely eats a bite. He won't invent bird toys now. He refuses to do any work in school too. He just sits there staring.

I want to shake him and scream in his face, "Invent something awful! Invent something great! Invent a new way of inventing." But of course, he has to mourn, even if I don't like it.

There was a little good news. It seems his Nan had signed custody over to Ms. Priscilla so he'd never end-up in a state home. So now she's his Step-mom in a way. Ms. Priscilla informed us that her mother and Ryan's Nan went to school together a long time ago.

He was also told that the savings his Nan left to the castle were put into a trust sort of thing. That the money was only used per month on his necessities, like food and clothes and doctors. That way there might be enough left once he's grown-up for him to go to college.

At least that made him stop crying. Yet the only time he's even sort of himself is when he's feeding or snuggling the birds. Joe seems to know something's wrong. Every day now he tells Ryan a secret, I think. He says, "Gurgle drip chirp" I dunno what that means but he only does it for Ryan.

Today as Ryan leaves for class, he stops and asks, "Aren't you coming?"

"No. I'm sick. Why are you going? You won't even read or anything."

"I'll tell the teacher you're sick," Ryan says flat. He slams the door.

No good.

I was trying to pick a fight maybe. I was trying to get a reaction.

Anything... anything to bring back Ryan to himself.

I am so angry I feel like I could just spit blood! Mrs. Krench had cancer. She lived.

Unfair, my gut screams.

My Mom has a Diffuse Axonal Injury. An actual factual brain injury. She lived.

Unfair, my heart thumps loudly.

Ryan's Nan only had pneumonia... Just a bad infection... But she died.

Unfair, my brain rages.

People live through pneumonia ... every... single... day! EVERY SINGLE DAY!

Unfair, Unfair, Unfair, my blood screams as it pulses.

The car my Mom was in was cut in half! She lived.

Unfair!

I have my Mom. Ryan hasn't got his Nan. Even though his Nan knew him. Loved him. Cherished him. Remembered him.

"Unfair," I start screaming. I can't stop for some reason, "Unfair! Unfair! Unfair! Unfair! Unfair!"

Ms. Priscilla opens the door to the roof just then, followed by a doctor.

I dunno what happened next. I was told they gave me something to help me sleep.

My screaming on the castle roof was something that Ms. Priscilla was concerned about. She'd even talked to my doctor and offered to call my Dad. I asked her not to. She told me that since the doctor said that I was healthy (other than stress) we didn't have to talk about it again, if I didn't want to.

I really don't want to. I'm afraid that everyone thinks I'm a loon now. And I also really believed that Ryan was mad at me for it.

It's been a month since Ryan's Nan passed. He's not himself. I was so worried that I made everything worse for him. Ryan seemed to be getting sadder. For a while I thought it was my fault. I felt so guilty about it, that I wouldn't give him a moment's rest. I just kept apologizing.

My continuous apologies, finally made him tell me everything. It turned out it wasn't me that made his mourning worse. He even said, "You're my bestest friend. Why would I get mad cuz you got sick and started yelling?"

So, then I needed to know exactly what had happened. I just couldn't leave it there. I pressed him and he told me everything. It turned out that a big kid called Ryan a great big loser because he cried at his Nan's funeral. So, Ryan believed it.

I made a bestest friend promise not to tell. But...

To be fair I never ever break promises. But to be fairer, somebody has to help Ryan and I don't know how. So, I blurted it out while we were in class. (I might be the worst friend ever, but I'm really scared for Ryan.)

I hear Ms. Priscilla say to Ryan, "You were sent here to begin with because you were bullied. Is that correct?"

Ryan says weak, "Yeah. I had a friend, well not really a friend, just a girl and her brothers. My Nan arranged that we would walk to the bus stop for school together. I'd get there really early but they didn't talk to me much. I usually just watched TV with their Dad until time to leave. They weren't bullies. They never hit me..."

"But they did something mean? Tell me. You're safe now," the teacher says.

"They teased me. Called me awful names. They wouldn't stand near me on the bus stop either... The girl, Corrine, told me she'd never be popular hanging around me. Because I was a loser."

"They bullied you with words," Ms. Priscilla explains.

"Everybody did. Lots of kids hit me. But it's cuz I was a loser. I didn't have the right clothes to be cool. I was always short. I was getting fat. I lived in a nasty neighborhood. I ... I deserved it." I hear Ryan's voice breaking and I want to hug him.

"Nobody deserves bullying, Ryan. And now you are more than all of those bullies combined."

"No. What do you mean?" Ryan says starting to cry again.

"Well, for one you live in a castle. Do they?'

"No."

"And you have learned to train birds. Do you think they can say that?"

"No... but that doesn't cancel loser," he weeps.

"No. You're right. It doesn't. Things and circumstance rarely define us. But you know what does?"

"What?"

"Kindness. You were afraid of the ravens and crows at first, but you didn't chuck a rock at them, because you have something a lot of people don't have… Empathy. You two thought that Mrs. Krench was a wicked witch… or so I overheard. But when she became ill you helped out in the kitchen. You did her chores. That is an amazing act of kindness, to help people you aren't fond of. Many people would've turned away, saying that helping her was inconvenient. You would be surprised at how many acts of evil have happened simply because helping another person is inconvenient. You are a good person and you've always been. Those bullies were dead wrong. There is nothing wrong with crying when someone dies, Ryan. It's quite natural."

"But they all said loser, all…"

"Ryan I can say the walls in this room are painted black. Does that make it true?"

"No. These walls are white."

"Well, that is impossible. You just told me that if someone says something, it's true. So, if I told you that these walls are painted black, it must also be true."

"No," Ryan replies, his face all scrunchy, "You must be confused. These walls are white."

"Exactly. As my grandmother used to say, paper lies still for anything to be written on it. What that means is that people can say anything. Anything at all."

"Oh." Ryan thinks for a minute.

"You're right. I understand now. Anyone can say whatever they want and still be wrong!" I hear Ryan say, but then he cries all over again, "Ms. Priscilla I really, really miss my Nan."

We both hug him so tight.

And in that sobby mess it seemed like our tears for him and our tears for ourselves made one whisper of true peace in our hearts.

*I know it's because we care about what happens to him. Even though we don't have to. Caring about others must be important because somehow it quiets that awful word, **unfair**.*

I guess I do like Ms. Priscilla afterall.

Ravens mate for life. They do not remarry.
(This is also true of their wolf companions.)

7
BIRD DOCTORS

Joe is acting really strange. Also, we haven't seen Paddy for a couple of weeks. We asked the teacher to come to the roof. We just asked in case they're getting sick or something. They must be.

I'm scared that my poor bird family got a brain injury. Their caws are totally different. They even move differently now. They get a funny strut and sort of bob. They puff up their feathers around their necks too. It's way weird.

There's hardly any caws or clicking now. I keep hearing, "Rwhoop. Whooop." They must be telling us they are sick and need our help.

"Is there such a thing as a bird doctor?" Ryan asked nervously.

"I never heard of one. But maybe there's doctors for everything these days." I reply. "It makes sense that if scientists are studying them, they must need to keep them healthy."

Joe flies and lands in front of Ryan with a loud, "ka-caw." Ryan gives him a piece of the hamburgers we had for lunch. Joe takes it but doesn't eat it. He just flies away and comes back a few minutes later.

Ms. Priscilla is now with us. She giggles. Ryan gets really upset.

"Why are you laughing? He's throwing away the food cuz he's sick. Paddy's not here either. He might be dead!" he yelps.

Ms. Priscilla giggles louder. She eventually catches her breath. She quips, "You have it all wrong. Your friend Paddy's a girl. She's sitting on a nest. She's laid a clutch." She giggles more.

"You mean Joe got married? To Paddy?" Ryan asks confused.

"Yes. Your friend Joe is taking his wife breakfast. He's about to be a daddy!"

"Marcy!" Ryan yelps jumping up and down, "Go to the kitchen. We need lots more food… and hot towels!"

"Oh," Ms. Priscilla still trying not to giggle says, "They don't need hot towels. But it is time to learn about their young. Ravens usually lay a clutch of 3-7 eggs. The babies hatch about three weeks later. Both parents feed the babies by regurgitating food and water that they store in their throat pouch."

"That sounds disgusting," I reply.

"Well, to be fair, they probably think that our baby bottles are disgusting," Ms Priscilla says, but you can see she's thinking.

"I'll tell you what, Ryan," she smiles, "Just this once we'll make them a mince pie. I think they'd be very grateful."

"What's a mince? Some kind of weird berry?" I ask.

"Mince… you know minced meat. It's meats that are ground and mixed." she explains.

"That's the worst pie I ever heard of," Ryan tells her.

"Well… That's because you're not a raven." she responds.

Feeding baby birds with an eye-dropper (as seen in movies) is very dangerous for the bird. Birds do not have an epiglottis, so it is more likely that the baby bird would drown. If you find a baby that has fallen from its nest or is injured, it is best to call your local bird rescue.

We are jumping out of our skin almost. The teacher told us it will only be about a month before Paddy brings their babies to meet us! They must grow fast. I used my free time in town and all of my allowance that I could save at the book store. I bought us a book of baby names.

Ariel is a good raven baby name. So is Oliver. All of the names seemed totally great for our new bird family. But since Ryan has to help me decide, I bought the book.

The cashier looked really confused for some reason.

Ms. Priscilla collected our papers on the crows and ravens. She even gave Ryan extra credit for his bird toy. It didn't work but it was a cool idea.

I'm thankful we have school in summer and winters off. I'm also happy it's second term. I'm really happy that I don't have to read ghost stories anymore. After Ryan's Nan died it seemed really gross to think about ghosts anyway. If they were real, he'd have seen his Nan again.

Mrs. Krench is back and we help her in the kitchen, but today I'm sad to say it'll only be her and Ryan. Most unfortunately Ms. Priscilla and I are going to visit my Mom.

I'm trying to think of anything I can to keep my mind off of seeing my mother. That doesn't work out too well.

I push the thought of my mom out of my head. I push the castle into my head again. That backfires because I was already really upset about it. We were told that by winter, that Rigby guy will probably buy the castle. It's so big and expensive.

But it's a castle. Can't someone make him stop?

Castles are not only in history, they're even in fairy-tales. Doesn't that make them double important?

I can't think about that now. I have much bigger problems today, I realize.

I don't know why I have to visit my Mother. I'm really angry before we even get to the hospital. I know she's had massive brain injury, but she forgot who I am, so I guess I wasn't very important.

There's always a tiny, little hope in me that I will walk into her room and she'll say my name.

Then I'd matter.

When we get to her room it's the same as always.

Her eyes light up and I get excited. But then I'm crushed. Mom says, "It was a summer day. There was an accident."

It's too much. Why doesn't she care enough to remember who I am? My throat feels acidy and gross. I scream at her, "I hate you!"

Crying, I run down the hall until I find some chairs in an empty lobby. Ms. Priscilla has run behind me. She sits next to me. She squeezes my hand.

At least she cares, I think, but I am broken angry. Sick angry. Bellyache angry.

"Remember when the raven brought you the stick?" she asks.

"Yes! It was great. She was saying thank-you for all the treats!" I smile, though I don't feel up to smiling.

"So, Paddy didn't speak, but you knew what she meant?" Ms. Priscilla asks, hands now fussing with the lace around her neck.

"Of course I knew. It was obvious," I reply.

"Yet your mother has suffered a massive brain injury and you can't talk to her?"

"She only ever says one thing. She doesn't care about me. She doesn't even remember me."

"Listen to me," Ms. Priscilla fusses, "A bird without a word can tell you things. But not your mother? She is only capable of saying one sentence, but you must treat it like a 'caw'... Some birds can only communicate with one or two noises, yet you understand them. Your mother has had a horrendous accident, that left her with only a 'caw.' Look past the words and see her."

"I know what you're saying but..."

"Marcy, if she only has one sentence then that sentence means everything. It's got to mean every single thing, mad, sad, happy... It's the only way she can express herself. She could be saying that she loves you and you'd miss it. She could be telling you that a terrible thing happened and that's why she can't say the words.

I'll tell you a secret. When I was young my mother and I didn't get along. I ran away and married a boy who soon left. She died a few months later. It destroyed me. I thought it was my fault. Love your mother while she's here. Love her before you run out of time. She can't say it, but she'll know it."

Something in my heart changes just then. I can hear the ravens and crows on the rooftop. I can hear them deep in my soul.

Just because Momma doesn't have a stick to give me, doesn't mean she's hateful. I think.

I march back down the hall and into her room. I get all my courage together and I say, "I love you bestest, Mom. I always will."

She replies, "It was a summer day. There was an accident."

Some part of me knows it means I love you.

Corvids are now known to be the smartest birds on earth, surpassing the previously considered African Gray Parrot.

8
Sink or Swim

I got really sick after my visit with Mom. I got filled with sharp-edges, tummy aches. I was even shaking. The doctor was called. He said it was just anxiety. He gave me something to put me to sleep. I don't think he has any other kind of medicine in his bag.

I skip seeing the birds this morning. I need to talk to my teacher, alone.

"The last thing I said to her… before the accident…" my voice trails off.

Maybe I shouldn't tell Ms. Priscilla…. But I can't tell Dad because he'd hate me forever. I have to tell someone. Because it hurts so much.

"Did you argue, Marcy?" Ms. Priscilla asks calm.

"Yeah," I admit after several minutes, "I wanted to go to Brandy's party at the lake-house. Mom, said I couldn't go because there weren't any adults there. I called her stupid. She got upset and wrecked the car!"

I am crying... No! I am wailing. I am wailing now. Tears are everywhere. Giant balls of sobs. It's like I could drown the whole world.

And I want to. I want to drown the world. If I do that I won't have to exist. I wouldn't have to feel. I wouldn't have to be responsible. I would never have to admit anything. Drown! Drown please!

But I can't make enough tears.

Unfair.

"Your father assured me that the other driver was responsible for that accident, Marcy. It wasn't your fault."

"Maybe so. But if she wasn't upset... she might have seen him coming! It is my fault!"

"Had you ever argued with your mother before that, Marcy?" she asks. Her face looks like a statue, etched in stone or something.

I think for a second. I screech, "Well of course. All the time!"

"Well, did she always treat you as if you were loved? After arguments? Did she love you anyway?"

"Yeah," I admit and something ugly inside me moves further away.

"She would be mad the whole day. But every night before I went to bed, she always told me that I was her sweet baby girl."

I feel something in me lift as I remember this, "Sweet baby girl."

"Marcy, that's a great, big clue, isn't it?" she says softly, "Not only was it not your fault, nobody blames you. That's something unnecessary that you're doing to yourself. Your mother has always loved you and she always will."

Still crying I yell, "I wished I knew before it happened. I wouldn't have yelled at her…"

"Marcy would you ever call a random stranger, stupid?"

"No. Of course not." I admit, "But that just makes it so much worse."

"People yell at the ones they love far more than they do at other people. We act out around our loved ones because we trust them to love us. Even when we are at our very worst, we know they have the strength to keep on loving us."

I've stopped crying but I still feel horrible, "I want to take it all back… but I can't."

"No. You can't. But you know what you can do? To make-up for it?"

I shake my head, "No"

"Just try to be a little kinder every day. To everyone. If you can become a better person every day (Even if it is just a tiny little bit) that is what is called a living amends."

I feel a lot better. I hug her and go to my room. I guess I still have tears for Momma. Since I won't drown, I guess I better try harder.

The time to sell the castle gets closer every single day. It's like being stuck in a door that closes tighter and tighter the longer you stay there.

Ryan and I did our best to save it. We handed out lots of fliers. We even got some books on the lost treasure from the library. But we never found it. I guess Mr. Headly's right. Somebody made the treasure story up so that treasure hunters would pay to get in.

I am so worried. Even though Ryan would still have Ms. Priscilla where would they live? And even Mrs. Krench and Mr. Headly? Where would they go? This was always their home. It's way worse than unfair. I'd have to go home... or probably to a girl's boarding school, which wouldn't have any ravens or crows. I hate that thought.

Ryan hates it more. He had Ms. Priscilla to help him write letters to the Historical Society. She also suggested the town council and the people that handle endangered wild life. I guess it was nice of her. Still... how are a couple of letters going to save a whole castle?

Anyways, none of those places ever wrote back.

I am picking up some apple peels and bits of meat that Mrs. Krench left for us to feed the birds.

Ryan bursts in. He's jumping up and down. He's flushed and looks redder than usual.

"The babies! The babies are here! Three of them!" he shouts.

We both run to the rooftop. Electric giggles fill us up. The only cure is seeing Joe and Paddy's babies! I don't think I've ever been this excited over anything in my whole life!

It's like I'm a grandma! No.

It's like I'm a step-mom. No.

It's like I'm a baby-sitter?

Whatever it's like... it's magic!

We see those fuzzy babies and we laugh. Blue-black fuzz is still visible in places. Ryan is running until I tell him to freeze. He stops and asks why.

"Those are their babies. Even if they can fly. I think Joe and Paddy probably don't want us near them so soon. I mean… parents are like that."

"Okay," he agrees, "Put the food down. Let them eat. We have to name them anyways. Plus, I think I fixed my bird toy. I'm saving it til they get bigger."

"But we don't know if they are girls or boys?" I say, "So how do we name them? Without insulting them, I mean?"

Ryan pulls the baby name book out of his pocket. He says, "Maybe we can find names that are the same for both. Like Pat."

"You wanna name one Pat?" I ask.

"No. But maybe… because Pat can be Patricia or Patrick." he replies with astonishing excitement.

"Oh, I see what you mean," I agree. The door to the roof opens. Everyone has come to see the babies. Ms. Priscilla comes towards us with another minced pie. She is followed by Mr. Headly and even Mrs. Krench.

Everyone ooohhs and ahhhs over the babies. But all the birds seem more interested in the mince pie.

Mr. Headly and Mrs. Krench leave to do their work, but Ms. Priscilla stays. She tells us, "Around here the first day of meeting baby birds is an automatic school holiday. Mr. Headly has even offered to take you into town."

"Ms. Priscilla, we want to name them with names that can be both boy and girl. But I can't find it in this book," Ryan tells her.

"Look in the table of contents for unisex." she replies.

Ryan goes completely red, "Ummmmm! You said a bad word!"

She giggles and simply tells him, "No it's not a bad word, Ryan. It means that the name can be used for either boys or girls."

Then she leaves giggling.

"Found it!" Ryan says. We spend an hour going through the names.

We decide on Ash, Avery and Dakota. (I decided on Dakota... The Dakotas were mentioned in my Indian School book.)

We are so busy with the book that we almost don't see the present that Paddy has brought us today to say thank you for the pie. Ryan looks up for a minute and yelps shrill, "Marcy? Is that what I think it is?"

I look up. It's miraculous! It's impossible!

Paddy drops a huge diamond ring at my side!

"The treasure!" we both shout! We are saved. But first we have to find it!

"I don't understand," Ryan whimpers, his face squinching up, "How can we follow Paddy? We can't fly."

He presses on a loose brick. It doesn't open a secret door. He presses another, not really looking at me. Nothing opens, no secret passages, and it really bugs me.

"Well..." I think for a while, "Maybe we can spend our free hours walking the grounds. We might get lucky."

"And if we don't?" he whines.

"Well... we know she's found it around the castle somewhere. We just aren't sure where. Maybe we should watch where they go."

"That seems like a good place to start, I guess. Why aren't we telling the grown-ups again?"

"They don't believe there's a treasure. They wouldn't want our hopes up," I say flat, "Might even give us more chores to keep our minds off of it."

"I don't think they would... well... Ms. Priscilla might give us essays on buried treasures!" he finally agrees.

All of this being very cloak and dagger would mean secret meetings, special missions and of course gathering intel (as I had explained to Ryan). He seemed starry-eyed but then demanded, "What's that mean? Gathering intel?"

"It just means that if you see something with the word intel painted on it you pick it up." I explain.

"Ooohhh." he starts walking away, pressing the wall again and again, but then he stops short. He turns, "What about the cloak and dagger part?" he asks.

"What about it?" I say.

"I have a cloak from Halloween, but why do we need a dagger?"

"I dunno. It doesn't matter. We'll start without one. We're too young to mess around with daggers anyway. So, we'll just have to use the cloak and hope for the best.... This is super-duper important!"

9
Cloak and Dagger Stuff

A week of meeting at night in the halls and discussing places that the treasure might be has not paid off. Every clue in the library books is a dead-end!

We spent an hour on our day-off. We were walking around moving small statues, but we never found any secret places. No treasure.... It makes me really mad.

I've watched the birds. I've seen the birds land all over the castle. Everywhere. How are we supposed to know which part has treasure if they just sunbathe everywhere?

I am so vicious mad right now! I could spit.

Ryan bursts into my room. He says happily, "I figured something out!"

"What's that?" I glower because I don't want him caught in here. We might be expelled.

"We can't use the library books to find the treasure… but we can!"

"You're talking nonsense. Do you have a fever?"

"No. Look," he grins, "All of the places in the books. They're all tales about people who looked for the treasure but never found it!"

"So?" I say wondering if I should tell someone to phone the doctor.

"That means the books only record where the treasure wasn't!" he yelps in an "aha" sort of tone.

I groan and Ryan nearly yells, "BUT we know from the books where there isn't treasure. We can cross those places off of our list! We can look in the other places instead!"

I nearly jump up.

"RYAN, YOU'RE A GENIUS!" I sort of shout. He turns and runs from the room, just in case I woke everyone up.

Expulsion would be bad luck for treasure hunting.

My Dad called again. He's been calling for a couple of weeks. I always pretend to be sick. I don't want him to tell me that I'm going to a different school because the castle is closing. If I just have a little more time we can find the treasure. I can't explain that either. It's a secret.

Ms. Priscilla as usual, sticks her nose in where it doesn't belong. She insists I take Dad's call. I still refuse.

I need more time. It's for Ryan.

Finally, Ms. Priscilla gets angry. It's scary when she's angry. She turns all purple and splotchy. She yelps, "Now you have been claiming for two weeks that you are too ill to speak to your father! So... you either go to the kitchen and talk to him OR I will drive you to hospital!"

I thought I liked her. Maybe I don't, I think.

"Why the hospital?" I nearly shout.

"If you've honestly been sick for this long then you need a visit to the emergency room!"

Now I'm angry too. I wonder if I also turn purple. I groan and stomp down to the kitchen.

I whine as I pick up the phone.

"Hello."

"Hi Ducky," Dad's voice says, "Heard you were sick."

"I'm okay now," I say. I don't feel like talking.

'Good! Marcy, something's come up that I think you ought to know about."

"Yeah," I reply, but I'm seething.

No I miss you? No I love you? Did he forget he's my Dad or something?

"It's about your Mom."

When he says that I hold my breath. My lungs might actually pop, but for some reason I can't exhale.

"Listen, the doctors want to do some surgeries. They might bring your mother back to herself. But the surgeries are very risky as well."

"Risky? Like dangerous?' I say but I am weeping.

"Yes, Ducky. Very dangerous. But they might help."

"WHY? Why would you let Mom be in danger? You don't love us anymore!" I yelp. Tears are everywhere again.

Drown. Please drown.

"Of course I love you both! You know your Mom was always a fighter. She never backed down from a challenge. Do you ever remember her walking away from a challenge?"

"No," I sniffle, "I remember we were both scared of rats. But when one chased me around the yard, she chased it off."

"Exactly," Dad agrees, "And because of that, I really think that if she could answer for herself... she'd agree to the surgeries. Even if it still took years of therapy... I think she'd try..."

"She would," I say and I hang-up the phone.

I wonder to myself why I even said that to him.

He can't know if she'd agree. How could anyone know that? She can't say yes or no. I can't say it for her. So, he can't either.

My stomach gets really sick just then. Suddenly in my mind I hear my Mom calling me her sweet baby girl... only in my head it isn't something she said before the accident. In my head it's something she says after the surgeries. I am smiling, crying, angry, confused, afraid and sad.

Maybe drowning isn't the answer. And maybe pretending I'm not scared for her is wrong. Because maybe deep down... just maybe... I'd rather have my Mom alive repeating two sentences, than in a coma or worse.

That thought frightens me so much that I am excused from class because Ms. Priscilla says I look sick.

We crossed those places in the book off of our lists. We've been searching all the rooms nobody uses. We were doing fine with the treasure hunt until Ryan opened his big, fat mouth to Mr. Headly!

He actually asked him if he could give us a dagger. Mr. Headly got really upset saying that something that dangerous isn't for kids. He further pressed Ryan as to why he wanted one and Ryan told him everything.

He even said, "We aren't having luck with just the cloak, so I really thought we needed a dagger to find the treasure."

I thought Mr. Headly was going to tell and we'd be expelled. I keep forgetting how nice he is.

"Aye," he said, "I looked for that treasure. Never found it, But if I catch either of you with ANY weapons I'll let your teacher know. You'll not like that."

"You're gonna tell?" I wince.

"Naw. But I ought to," he replied, "I'll keep yer secret long as ye both stay away from weapons and such. Every kid's a treasure hunter, I suppose. If ya do find need for a dagger, you'll be askin' me to use it for ya."

"We promise!" I yell merrily.

"Wait," Ryan says, "I don't understand."

"If'n ya'll find anything that needs dug up, or anything, I mean ANYTHING dangerous. Ye don't do it yourselves. Ya come ask me. Yeah? Otherwise, I'm tellin' your teacher you ain't being safe."

"Expulsion?" Ryan whimpers.

"Yep! And in my opinion expulsion ain't even enough of a punishment for foolishness that gets ya hurt!"

We make an oath. Best of all, we sort of have help looking for the treasure.

10
Ryan's Ravens

Ryan has been studying the Medieval period for History. Ms. Priscilla is actually a good teacher. She knows that Ryan is more interested in how things work than he is in wars and crops and stuff. She's pretty cool to teach him a sort of history about mechanisms. I never knew any teacher that taught like that.

Also, if we ask a question about something she shows us how to research it. It becomes another subject in class, but a fun one. It's very strange. It's like we both learned how to like homework now.

That can't be normal.

Today we were walking the castle grounds. I love learning about plants. Ms. Priscilla gave us a book about botany and a list of plants and flowers. We have to find them on the grounds for homework today. The really cool thing is that tomorrow she's going to show us how to press them and make a scrap book.

I'm super excited too. I just found a wild flower!

"LOOK!" Ryan yells. It scares me so bad I jump.

"What?" I screech.

"Look. Paddys just flew up to the roof!"

"So what?"

"Before that she was over at the side. By the ground."

"So?'

"Let's look there." he quips "Birds like shinny things!" And I agree.

We run as fast as we can to the spot where she'd been. When we get there, we can't see any opening. I grumble something under my breathe. I snap, "No fair. I was so excited too."

"There's a way in even if we don't see it," he says.

"Ryan, what are you talking about?" I grouch.

"She found a way in. So there has to be one. Let's go over there in the trees and watch her."

I really think it's a stupid idea but I go along with it. It turns out to be an excellent idea. A few minutes later Paddy returns. She lands behind a couple of big rocks and she disappears. She flies out a few minutes later with something shiny in her beak! We can see the flash of it in the sunlight.

"She's got a necklace or something." I yell victoriously.

"Yeah," Ryan says, "The book I got says they like to take shiny things into their nests. All we have to do to find the treasure is climb over the rocks."

So, Ryan without another word runs to where the rocks are. He climbs over and I follow. We see a small window at the very bottom of the castle wall. It has rusted bars across it. The bars are broken off in places. They're rusty and gross. Still, they are the most beautiful sight I've ever seen.

"It's a secret room under the castle!" Ryan yells happily.

"But if we can't find a door to it? I mean we've walked all over this place. I've never seen a door." I wince.

"Me either," he moans, "We can't ask Mr. Headly to go in and see if it's safe, until we can find the door."

In the middle of studies Ryan blurts out, "Ms. Priscilla? When we first toured the castle, we were shown a watery place. A little space where people kept their food cold?"

"That was how they kept food fresh! Fairly ingenious," she replies.

"Yeah... but there was a little door under it. We could see it," he says very far away.

"We believe there were mountain rocks kept under it. When water runs down a mountain the water is cleaned perfectly. We believe that they were trying to clean the water... to make it safe to drink."

"Maybe..." he trails off, "but did anybody open it? Did anybody check?"

"No. The door had rusted shut. Why do you ask?"

My eyes light up and I make a tiny squeal.

Ryan's just found the treasure!

We are inside the castle looking at the water under the little door.

I can't believe they used this for keeping food from spoiling. I hate wet groceries, I think.

"But there's water in it," I argue, "We can't even open the door underneath the water and look inside of it because the water is in the way. Even if we open the bottom door, all the water will just flood it forever. It's from the stream it's just going to keep flowing."

"Dam it," Ryan says plain.

"Watch your mouth!" I tell him. I know he's angry but….

"No," he responds, "I mean to dam it. To put up a barrier so the water stops. It's in one of my books."

"I dunno, Ryan. Why would they put the door to the treasure there? Then put water over the top? They wouldn't be able to get their gold and stuff."

"Because nobody ever looks there. But there must be…" his voice trails, "a switch … or dial..."

I see him grabbing at the candles and books. I see him moving vases.

He's looking for something I realize.

He's grabbing the edge of a tapestry. Next, he starts grabbing at any and everything on the wall of the castle. He starts to pull at the mounted sticks that were once used for torches.

When he starts pulling the mounted torches, I'm worried that they could fall on him. He's looking at the bottom of each torch. He runs his fingers up the sides. Suddenly he stops.

He turns to me, looking redder than usual. He yelps, "This one! This torch is different than the others. It has a silver trim on the bottom."

"So?" I sputter but I am amazed as Ryan pulls at the torch with all his might. There's a weird creaky sound. A tiny brick wall drops out of nowhere, closing off the small room under the floor. It blocks the flow of water. The continuous stream of water stops. The door can be opened now!

We are both jumping up and down!

"Go get Mr. Headly!"

11
Stairway to Heaven?

After Mr. Headly used his crowbar to pry open the little door he shined his flashlight into the very dark place under the door. There was a staircase under it. The entrance was really small. It was such a small opening that Ryan volunteered to go down first.

"Naw," Mr. Headly said, "Ain't no way to know if it's safe. Might even got structure damage after all this time."

"WE HAVE TO!" Ryan yelped.

"No! Ya promise me you'll leave off," Mr. Headly insisted, "I'll go into town in the morn. I got me a couple friends that can help me bring up this floor. We can make it safe. Might take a coupla weeks."

"But I heard Mrs. Krench say that rich guy is coming tomorrow! We don't have time!" Ryan nearly cries.

"Aye he is," Mr. Headly said, "But even if'n he tries to buy it, all of that bank paperwork's gonna take time. Don't you worry."

We go very sadly quiet as Mr. Headly scratches his beard. He adds, "Strangest thing today."

"What was strange?" I ask.

"After all of these years... a lass called. Said she were from that Historical Society. They weren't never interested before."

I see Ryan's face light-up "My letter! They read my letter!"

Maybe despite that mean Mr. Rigby, we might win after all.

My Mom had her first surgery today. The doctors said there's no change.

A very big secret:

Sometimes I hate her for being hurt.

Sometimes I hate Dad for trying to fix her.

But mostly I hate myself for hating them both.
Unfair.

What a weird, noisy week! Mr. Headly and his friend Tom are forever banging, pounding and drilling. It's set my teeth on edge. It's funny to me that nobody ever asks Mr. Headly what he's doing. He does so many repairs that everyone just thinks that that's what he's always doing. I guess that's good in the treasure hunting department. Ms. Priscilla simply said, "Mr. Headly has a right to do whatever he sees fit."

And that was such a strange thing to say, but that was the end of the conversation. Mostly because Ryan kicked me under the table.

The lady, Mrs. Burns from the Historical Society showed up this morning without any notice. She sort of barged in. She spent what must've been 2 hours with Ms. Priscilla looking at every inch of Castle Keep. She told her that it's a Historical building, but also that it could take up to a year to make certain that nobody knocks it down. She gave Ms. Priscilla some papers and left.

Next, some weird looking man with big thick glasses and binoculars shows up. He and Ms. Priscilla chatted too low for us to hear. But before we know it the teacher instructs us to show this man, Mr. Val to the roof to see the birds.

Why does he need to see them? He looks really weird to me.

We show the man to the roof. But I'm a bit embarrassed. The birds have been being really mean lately.

Dakota is bigger than Paddy now. The two peck at each other a lot. They even fight. It doesn't end until Dakota makes a very soft sort of "Who-hop wop" sound.

And of course they are doing this today, right in front of Mr. Val.

"Sorry," I say, "They only just started fighting. They never used to."

"Perfectly normal," he says using his binoculars to see all of the grounds.

"It isn't. They never used to fight. They just keep pecking each other."

"Uhuh," he says, "That's the pecking order. It makes the structure of the bird community."

"What are you talking about?" Ryan asks his face all scrunchy.

"One bird wants to be the leading bird, like the queen in this case. The younger wants to take over and make the first leader submissive. The older raven wants to keep her place as queen. So she will fight with the other until it gives up and makes that whooping sound you hear. That sound means, 'I surrender." says Mr. Val.

"Wow," I say stunned, "I didn't even know they had leaders."

"Well, every group in Nature's world must follow some law for survival. It's the leaders who not only make but must enforce and follow that natural law, in order to ensure survival. It's what keeps the DNA going."

He keeps looking through his binoculars and not at us.

"How do you know all this stuff?" Ryan asks.

"Exemplary!" he tells us, "Truly exemplary. I think this place will do nicely."

"What?" I yelp.

"You're trying to buy the castle?" Ryan squeaks.

"Nothing of the sort," he assures us, "That forest being federally protected for wolves, legally makes the sky from there to here a bird sanctuary."

"So, nobody can hurt them?" I ask.

"We will see. I'll have to report my findings. If it were up to me, this castle would stand as a protected nesting ground. Unfortunately, I'm not in charge." And then he just leaves.

12

BULLY

When that mean Mr. Rigby showed-up we were really upset. Ryan and I stood behind the stairwell wall so we wouldn't be seen. Mrs. Krench answered the door. She told the man flat, "No tours today!" and started to close the door.

Mr. Rigby became rude and started shouting. Ms. Priscilla walked up to the doorway. We were worried what might happen next. That guy Rigby was really mad. We thought he was going to hit someone. We were way scared.

Ms. Priscilla was calm and she did the strangest thing. She handed him a piece of paper. She said, "This may be of interest. That's the Historical Society."

The man started shouting again. Ms. Priscilla handed him another paper, "The University claims it may also be a bird sanctuary."

He was howling mad and really terrifying. He ripped up the papers and opened his mouth to yell again. Ms. Priscilla said flat, "So you see all of this must be discussed and cleared up with the owner of the estate. Otherwise, there can be no sale."

The man seemed a little calmer until Ms. Priscilla said quite loudly, "I'm afraid the estate owner is out. Please phone on Monday for an appointment. Good day."

And then she just closed the door. Right in his awful, screaming face!!

I saw Ryan's eyes light-up. He got a huge smile when the door slammed shut. I bet I have one too. I think he just figured out that bullies aren't as big as they pretend to be.

Closing the door in his face! That was like a super-power, I think.

That man was the biggest bully I ever saw. Yet Ms. Priscilla just closed the door. And it was over.

WOW!

This is a weird place to live. Fall's coming. All the trees are changing color. I never knew that that happened in real life. I thought it was made-up for post cards.

Mom had her second surgery today. Dad called to tell me. He said the doctors are very hopeful. He says it will take a lot of therapy, but that Mom might be herself again someday.

I can't keep that in a happy place in my heart. Because if I get my hopes up…

I mean what if it doesn't work?

I can't bear to think about it. So, I just don't. Good or bad, I just don't.

We are all standing squished together in the doorway. Mr. Headly and his friend took the time to rebuild the stairway so it would be safe. Giant battery-operated lanterns light the rather scary-looking hall down to the next landing.

When we get down there, our hearts nearly break! There is a door blocking a larger room. There's a gigantic iron lock on it!

"Oh no!" Ryan yelps, "We'll never find the key. It's been down here too long."

Mr. Headly laughs. He steps up to the locked door. He reaches into the back-pocket of his jeans and pulls out a huge wrench. He slams the wrench on the lock really hard a few times, but it doesn't budge.

"We'll never get in!" I whine.

"'Course we will. We ain't come all this way for nothin'" Mr. Headly says. He turns around and heads back up the stairwell.

"Why's he leaving?" Ryan asks Ms. Priscilla.

"Because he needs a different tool, I would think," she replies, but then she adds, "I hope you two will not be completely disappointed if there is no treasure behind that door."

"There HAS to be!" I insist, "We looked everywhere else!"

"Mr. Headly made it quite clear that the treasure rumor was probably made-up to bring in tourists," she replies.

"There has to be treasure!" Ryan winces, "We looked so hard. Besides, what else could be back there?"

"I don't know, Ryan," Ms. Priscilla admits, "Could just be an old coat room... or even a spinning room where the woman made clothe."

My heart falls into my toes.

What if she's right? What if we tried so hard and didn't find anything except another room! Ryan would be heartbroken. So would I!

If we lose the castle we might lose each other.

All of us living apart?

Unfair!

I have to stop thinking about it. I feel really sick now.

Mr. Headly comes back down the stairs. It feels like he's been gone forever. He has a canvas bag in his hands. He gives each one of us a small flashlight.

He has used his belt as a holder for a giant pair of lock-cutters. He smiles and grabbing them, he tells us, "I knew I were gonna need these someday."

He moves to cut the lock, but Ryan stops him, "Mr. Headly I'm really sorry if it turns out you built all of these stairs and there's no treasure."

I almost start crying at how sweet Ryan says that.

You can tell he really means it.

Mr. Headly begins laughing, "Any history is treasure. Don't matter if it be gold or just old things. They all tell us somethin' worth knowin' Don't they?'

Ryan nods, but you can tell he really wants there to be treasure inside.

Me too!

Finally, we hear a heavy sort-of grinding sound, then a clank. The old lock falls on the floor. The door begins to open with an awful SCRITCH... creak.

Mr. Headly shines his light in first. A glimmer sort-of echoes back. I can hear Ryan holding his breathe. That's when I realize that I'm holding mine too.

"Stay there," Mr. Headly warns, "I'll go first. Make sure that there floor's solid."

We are standing waiting for him to return for what seems like a century. Suddenly his face shows back at us through the door. He says, "Floor's a good solid stone... but I gotta warn ye kids..."

Now everyone is holding their breath. I know because I can feel it in my own chest.

"Ya found it!" Mr. Headly crows, "Ye two kids found that treasure of Castle Keep!"

Everyone cheers so loud that I bet people can hear it two countries away!

We all step into the room, flashlights searching for gold. Mr. Headly steps out and brings a couple of the huge lights in from the stairway.

As the light spreads across the room, we can't believe our eyes. The treasure takes up an entire room. Gold, diamonds, rubies, silver… every shiny thing ever! It's stacked to the roof in places.

We are all touching the treasure, sort of playing dress-up with the jewelry.

Ryan pulls something shiny out of a pile and puts it on his head. He yelps, "Look! A crown!"

"No," I tell him, "It's a tiara."

"What's the difference?" he asks.

"It's for a girl," I tell him. He puts it back and pulls out something else. Looks like a chain of some kind. He studies it with his flashlight.

He asks, "What are these blue stones in this necklace?"

Ms. Priscilla looks and says, "My guess would be sapphires, but they could be blue diamonds."

"Diamonds come in blue?" I ask.

"Certainly, black, yellow. Diamonds do in fact come in most colors!" she answers.

"Well... then how do you even know if they're diamonds?" I ask. But Ryan cuts me off with a loud squeal.

"The castle is saved! We can pay off the debt!" Ryan cheers, and I'm glad he says it. I was so starry-eyed that I almost forgot what we were doing down here.

"That's entirely up to Mr. Headly," Ms. Priscilla quips.

"Whatdya mean?" I ask.

We could still lose the castle? I don't understand.

"It's Mr. Headly's decision," Ms. Priscilla says, "The treasure was found on his premises. So, it really belongs to him."

"MR. HEADLY?" me and Ryan yelp, "Mr. Headly owns Castle Keep?"

"Aye. I did, til I got into debt. Me ancestral home." he tells us.

"But why don't you dress rich and stuff?" I ask without thinking.

He's quiet a moment. Then he says, "It's good ya kids found the treasure. I won't have to lose this old place. Still... treasures ain't the true riches.

The true treasure is a hard day's work, a job well done. I like knowin' those that came before me know I'm keepin' the place up. Mendin' the roof my great great granddads was under. Fixin' cracks in the walls of rooms that my grannies lived in. That's the treasure. It ain't the family home. It's the family."

That hits me really hard! It almost breaks my heart into a thousand pieces for some reason.

I realize, *My family matters more than anything. As they are right now. As they will be in the future. Good or bad. Healthy or ill. None of those things really matter… just as long as they are my family.*

I say sniffling, "Ms. Priscilla, I want to visit my Mom… as soon as the doctors say it's okay.

A flock of crows is called, "A murder".
A flock of ravens is called an "unkindness."

*Ravens (even as adults) play games together.
Many have been seen tossing small rocks to one another
in mid-air as if they are playing ball.*

13

ALL GOOD THINGS

I'm so glad we get winter off. It's been months since Mr. Headly bought the castle outright. There's been snow here and everything. I never saw snow before this.

It's been so cool because apparently ravens and crows both play in the snow! They look so funny doing it! Some dive, some roll but they all look funny.

Ryan taught me how to make snowballs and how to build snowmen. We don't go out every day. But we still feed the birds every day. Dakota's been gone for months. Ms. Priscilla said sometimes they decide to live in another flock, and that maybe Dakota's got a crush on another bird. We giggled at that.

That weird man, Mr. Val visits regularly but nobody minds. He goes up to see the birds but every time before he leaves, he ends up spending an hour talking to Ms. Priscilla. I think he may have a crush on Ms. Priscilla and all.

But today is the best day, the day of all good things. Today is Christmas!

The ravens must know it's Christmas. They landed today and their 'Caws' seemed ever so jolly. Joe brought us a sprig of mistletoe. (I think he stole it from the wreath on the front door.)

It was strange that Mr. Val showed-up because he doesn't live here. I don't know if he was actually invited, but he brought gifts. He got Ms. Priscilla a pair of binoculars, and he got me and Ryan each a book called "Corvids" that his university wrote. It was too hard to read, with really big words... but the pictures were great!

Mrs. Krench made us gingerbread cookies and taught us to make s'mores in the fireplace. Ms. Priscilla gave us each a leather-bound book and a nice pen set so we can write diaries for the birds in a proper fashion. Mr. Headly got us each new winter coats and he brought in some of those little cars that you pull back and they go. Him and Ryan were racing the plastic cars and giggling all morning.

Suddenly Ms. Priscilla calls everyone to attention. She brings in a giant wrapped box with my name on it. I see Ryan looking around. He didn't get one. He looks really sad.

"Open it!" Ms. Priscilla instructs. And I do. But as I tear away the paper, I feel kind of guilty.

Why didn't Ryan get a big gift too? That's so mean.

I open the box, there's nothing in it.

"It's empty." I snort.

"No. Look closer," Ms. Priscilla says.

I look again. There's a little slip of paper in it. I grab the paper and open it.

"It says, Answer the door." I read aloud. Suddenly the doorbell rings. I run to pull it open. I nearly faint.

My dad is standing there! My Dad! But even more amazing, he is pushing Mom in a wheelchair.

They came for Christmas! They do love me!

I gasp. I hug them.

Dad finally tells me, "I got another job to be with your Mom through all her therapy. The hospital's only a mile away."

"What? You're staying here?" I ask.

"We're staying. All of us!" he tells me, "A man named Mr. Headly contacted me, he said there was a small wing of the castle, five large rooms here that nobody uses. He welcomed us to move into it. So… this is our home now!"

Everyone is jumping up and down.

Mr. Headly walks into the room dressed like Santa. He looks just like him. I giggle. He's carrying a huge bag.

"Ho ho ho! Who wants toys and sweeties?" he asks and everyone rushes to him.

I smile a smile so wide that it probably doesn't even fit on my face. My heart giggles! I've never felt so wonderful!

I think I have happy tears. I don't know if I really want anyone to notice. So, I walk to the big window and look outside.

The birds are playing in piles of fluffy, white snow. They are happily plopping themselves into a small snow bank.

I see Joe and Avery diving into the snow. The snow sorta splashes up and falls back down. Joe has snow on his head now. I start to giggle. He looks so funny.

I see Paddy, Hadley and Ash watching them from a tree. I watch as they dive next. They all seem so happy. You can see the love of a family there. And it feels just like all of the love in my heart.

Would I have found that love? Without those birds? Without these wonderful people?

We ARE a family! Me, my parents... ALL of us! Mr. Headly, Ryan, Ms. Priscilla... even Mrs.

Krench! Joe and all of our birds too! Maybe even Mr. Val! Family isn't made of blood. A real family is made of heart!

Sometimes a bad time is replaced by a miracle. Most of the time, those miracles are other living things.

The End

Caged birds (in your home) should not be released into the wild. This is because birds raised in captivity have not learned to forage. Finding food is a skill that is taught by other birds in the wild when they are babies.

ABOUT THE AUTHOR

ANGEL DUNWORTH is an award-winning author and artist. Writing is unquestionably her first love, having won her first writing accolade by the 4th grade. She says of this, "I've always made-up stories, but winning that school competition certainly lit a fire under me." Her passion for the written word and her love for all things creative, reflect not only in her writing but also in her illustrations.

She's been published in many literary collections. Her work regarding the topic of Vietnam is archived in one of the many, Wall Museums. She also has a free Virtual Textbook, available on you-tube, for homeschoolers that teaches literary tools.

Dunworth currently resides in Windcrest, Texas, with her husband who she proclaims, "Is the love of my life!"

www.ingramcontent.com/pod-product-compliance
Lightning Source LLC
Chambersburg PA
CBHW051347040426
42453CB00007B/449